Have a
New Kid
by Friday

Participant's Guide

Have a New Kid
by Friday

PARTICIPANT'S GUIDE

How to Change Your Child's
Attitude, **B**ehavior & **C**haracter
in **5 Days**

A Six-Session Study

Dr. Kevin Leman

Revell

a division of Baker Publishing Group
Grand Rapids, Michigan

© 2013 by Dr. Kevin Leman

Published by Revell
a division of Baker Publishing Group
P.O. Box 6287, Grand Rapids, MI 49516-6287
www.revellbooks.com

Printed in the United States of America

Library of Congress Cataloging-in-Publication Data

Leman, Kevin.
    Have a new kid by Friday participant's guide : how to change your child's attitude, behavior & character in 5 days (a six-session study) / Dr. Kevin Leman.
        pages cm
    ISBN 978-0-8007-2175-6 (pbk.)
    1. Discipline of children. 2. Discipline of children—Religious aspects—Christianity. 3. Parenting. 4. Parenting—Religious aspects—Christianity. I. Title.
    HQ770.4.L434 2013
    248.8'45—dc23   2013000141

16   17   18   19   20   7   6   5   4   3

Contents

How to Use This Participant's Guide   6

Want a New Kid by Friday? *Take this quick quiz.*   9

Introduction

They're Unionized . . . and Growing Stronger   11

Monday

Where Did They All Come From?   20

Tuesday

Disarming the Dude (or Dudette) with the 'Tude   29

Wednesday

Show Me a Mean Teacher, and I'll Show You a Good One (It's All in the Perspective)   38

Thursday

But What If I Damage Their Psyche? (Uh . . . What's a Psyche?)   47

Friday

The Doc Is In . . . and It's You   55

Epilogue: It's Time to Launch   65

Appendix 1: Have a New Kid by Friday Plan for Success   67

Appendix 2: The Top 10 Countdown to Having a New Kid by Friday   69

About Dr. Kevin Leman   71

Resources by Dr. Kevin Leman   72

How to Use
This Participant's Guide

Here's the most important thing you need to know: this is *your* participant's guide. That means you can use it in any way that works best for you and your group. Every individual and group is unique, and only by trying new things will you find out how this guide works best in your group. So do whatever brings you and your group the maximum impact.

Each of the six sessions is set up in the following basic format.

The Kickoff

Questions to launch group interaction and promote sharing.

Watch

Scenes from *Have a New Kid by Friday DVD*.

Discuss the DVD

Questions to connect the DVD material to your everyday life.

Taking It Deeper

Questions, reflections, and insights to aid your transition to having a new kid by Friday.

Remember

Bite-size nuggets of wisdom to carry with you.

My Game Plan for Today

What to do to reach your goal—having a new kid by Friday.

Aha Moments

Space to record your insights and thoughts from the day's session. For additional reflection, start a separate journal of "Aha Moments."

Prayer

A time to commit your goals to God, pray for others in the group, and ask God for his help in giving you the determination to stick to your plan.

The structure of the first session, "Introduction," will be slightly different from the Monday through Friday sessions because it's just that—an introduction. In the Friday session, the discussion sections are shorter to allow for the additional reading of "It's Time to Launch" and to review "Have a New Kid by Friday Plan for Success" as a group. You may also choose to have a lengthier prayer time in this last session.

Now that you understand the basic format, you can be creative and experiment. Here are some ideas to get you started.

- The "Want a New Kid by Friday?" quiz can be taken by group members either on their own before the group starts (to shorten the length of the first session), or where noted in "Introduction."

- Use "The Kickoff" questions either before or after you watch the video clip. For sessions two through six, individuals can come prepared with their responses to the opening questions, if so desired.

- Watch the full video clip altogether, or pause it to discuss the DVD questions or "Aha Moments" you are getting from watching the video.

- The "Remember" section is a great summary or reminder of the main points of each session. You as a group member could compile a six-page "Remember" book, adding a new page at the end of each session that includes those bulleted points and highlights of your own "Aha Moments." A "Remember" book will be an encouraging reminder of the key principles and insights you've gained as you've walked through this participant's guide. It will strengthen your resolve in those difficult moments of being a parent (and we all have them).

- "My Game Plan for Today" can be done during the group session—by breaking into one-on-one conversations or through individual reflection time—or as follow-up individual journal time after the session. As a further reminder, write your note highlights on an index card and carry it in your wallet or purse. (Hint: Don't post it on the fridge where your kids can see it and know what you're up to.)

- Share your "Aha Moments" in your group discussion at the end of each session, or at the beginning of the next session, when you've had time to reflect on them. Or those moments can be private ones, noted in your participant's guide or journal.

- For the prayer time, try a variety: prayer with the whole group, one-on-one, or with three to four people, or write a private prayer in your journal. Use the prayer suggestions as prompts for your prayer time, or allow God's Spirit to move your group to pray for specific needs, as desired. Be mindful that some people in your group may not be persons of faith or might be uncomfortable praying audibly. Let everyone know they don't have to contribute a prayer.

See how this works? The sky is the limit on how you can use the materials.

Regarding leadership, some groups have an appointed leader. If that works for you, great! But if none of you like the idea of being the leader, then why not share leadership? Have members take a turn leading the group. Anyone who can push the button to start the DVD, read questions, and invite others to share and pray can be a leader. Or you might want to have two individuals share the responsibility for a session—one to start and stop the DVD and another to ask the questions. It really is just that simple . . . and easy.

Above all, take advantage of this practical, hands-on participant's guide that will transform your family's life and help you get that new kid by Friday. And along the way, you'll have a lot of fun too!

I guarantee it.

Want a
New Kid by Friday?

Take this quick quiz. Simply mark Y for Yes or N for No on the line before each entry.

About You

___ Do you expect the best of your child?

___ Do you mean what you say?

___ Do you follow through on what you say?

___ Do you hold your child accountable for his or her actions?

If you're four for four with all "Y" answers at this point, stick around. The rest of those in the group are going to need you for a mentor.

___ Do you yell at, scream at, threaten, or cajole your child to do simple, routine things like get up for school, get dressed, eat, do homework, or perform a chore?

___ When you say no to your child and your child cries, are you overcome by guilt? Do you find yourself giving in to the original request of your child—saying yes to what you had just said no to?

___ Do you engage in long conversations with your child, defending why you said no to a certain request?

___ Are you worried that your child doesn't feel good about himself or herself?

___ Are you bothered that your child doesn't seem happy?

___ Do you plan over-the-top birthday parties?

___ Are you concerned about your child not keeping up with the successes or achievements of other children?

___ Have you ever wished another child would fail so your child would look better?

___ Do you have a difficult time saying no?

___ Do you have a hard time saying to your child what you really feel as a parent?

___ Are you frustrated most days?

About School

___ Are you overly involved in your child's life? Do you fear that something terrible will happen if you don't chaperone every school field trip?

___ Do you complete your child's school assignments and projects?

___ Do you require a full explanation from your child's teacher when your child doesn't receive a superior grade?

___ Do you make excuses for your child not having completed his or her assignments on time? ("Oh, it was our fault. We had to go to_____ and we had_____ to do.")

___ Does a simple homework assignment take the whole family's energy for an entire evening? Are the end results lots of tears and frustrations—and an assignment that either never gets done or doesn't get done right?

___ Do you check and correct homework on your child's behalf?

About Your Children

___ Do they have to be asked to help around the house on a daily basis?

___ Do they disrespect you and not value what you have to say?

___ Do they fuss about obeying you?

___ Do they lack for nothing?

___ Are they engaged in one or more extracurricular activities?

___ Do they need to be reminded more than once to do something?

___ When they slam the door in your face, do you write it off as "just the way kids are"?

___ Is bedtime a battle zone?

If *any* of these topics resonated with you and you marked even one "Y," you're in the right group.

This participant's guide will scratch where you itch.

I promise.

Introduction

They're Unionized . . . and Growing Stronger

> Your kids have a game plan to drive you bonkers. But you don't have to let them call the shots. I've got a game plan guaranteed to work. Every time.

Your kids have a game plan to drive you bonkers. It all started back with Eve birthing two brothers—Cain and Abel—who were as different as day and night and couldn't get along. And we all know how that story ended up.

There's always at least one kid in your home who is determined to go a certain direction—a direction you don't want him or her to go. What's worse, your kids are unionized . . . and growing stronger. In today's society, children even shorter than a yardstick are calling the shots. They're part of what I call the "entitlement group"—they expect anything and everything good to come their way, with no work on their part, just because they exist. In their eyes, the world (and Mom and Dad) *owes* them. Some of them are part of the ankle-biter battalion; others have graduated to emeritus status and are holding down the hormone group division.

You know all about that, because that's why you've picked up this guide. It isn't always the big things that wear you down and make you say, "I've had it!" It's the constant battles with attitudes and behaviors like eye rolling, talking back, fighting with siblings, giving the silent treatment, and slamming doors. It's the statements like, "You can't make me do it!" and "I hate you!" flung in your face.

If you want to see some things—or a lot of things—change in your house, and you long for a better way of doing life in your home, *Have a New Kid by Friday Participant's Guide* and the accompanying DVD will help you accomplish just that. The principles are simple. Anyone can follow them. But they're not easy. They take willpower—yours. No wimps allowed. However, the payoff will be greater than you could ever imagine.[1]

The Kickoff

1. How many children do you have, and what are their ages?

2. If you could change just one thing about your interactions with your kids, what would that be? Why?

Watch

Watch "Introduction" on *Have a New Kid by Friday DVD.*

Discuss the DVD

1. When Dr. Leman said you could have a new kid not only by Friday but even by Wednesday, what was your gut-level response? Did you believe it? Why or why not? On what experiences do you base your answer?

1. If you haven't yet taken the *"Want a New Kid by Friday?"* quiz (pp. 9–10), do so now. If you wish to share your responses during group time, terrific! Otherwise, it's fine to keep them to yourself.

2. When have your kids starred in their own "dog and pony show"? Explain. How did you respond then? How might you handle your children's upcoming dog and pony shows differently?

3. If you're married, do you and your spouse tend to be on the same page in your interactions with your children? Or is one of you pulling one direction and the other another? How might pulling together in the same direction benefit your kids—and your marriage?

   If you're divorced, how might you and your ex (if your ex is still involved in your children's lives) both take a step in the same direction for the benefit of your children?

   If you're a single parent, how might you gather a support group of like-minded people around you?

4. Can you identify a recent situation where your child viewed reward as his or her right? What did your child say? How did you respond?

5. Should that situation come up again with your child, what might you do differently, knowing what you know from Dr. Leman?

Taking It Deeper

Nothing in life is a free ride, and the sooner your children learn that, the better. Each person is accountable, regardless of age, for what comes out of his or her mouth. And homes should be based on the cornerstones of mutual respect, love, and accountability. There is no entitlement. If you play the entitlement game in your home, you'll create BratZ—with a capital Z.

1. What adjectives would you use to describe the way you feel after doing battle with your kids?

2. Do your kids usually get what they want—and when they want it? Or do they have to save for an item they want, wait to go to a friend's house, etc.? Explain.

3. How has trying to make your kids happy upped the ante on their requests? On your stress level?

4. Imagine saying no to such requests. Paint the scenario of what would happen between you and your child.

5. Imagine not only saying no but sticking to that no, even when your child pleads for a change of heart. Now paint the scenario.

6. If you stick to your no, what do you think will happen the next time your child plays the entitlement game?

7. Philippians 2:3 says, "Do nothing out of selfish ambition or vain conceit, but in humility consider others better than yourselves." How might believing in and acting upon these words transform your family's interactions?

8. If your child didn't turn in a paper on time, what would you do—and why? For example:
   - Call the teacher to apologize that your daughter didn't get the paper in on time, and ask for an extension. Then push your daughter to finish it that night. (End result: your daughter screams at you and slams her bedroom door; you get angry and then feel bad.)
   - Email the teacher and tell her it's your fault—your daughter has had too full of a schedule—and ask for an extension. Then write the paper yourself that night so your daughter can turn it in the next day.
   - Write a note to the teacher and drop it off at school: "My daughter is late again on handing her paper in, and she has no excuse. I'd be grateful if you would give her the maximum deduction in her grade for lateness so she'll understand there are consequences to her actions."

9. Do you tend to snowplow your kid's road in life—making too many decisions for her, giving him too many choices, letting her off the hook, or making excuses when he's irresponsible? If so, what has been the result in your child's life and in yours?

10. Ecclesiastes 5:19 says, "When God gives any man wealth and possessions, and enables him to enjoy them, to accept his lot and be happy in his work—this is a gift of God." What is the source of happiness in this verse? How does trying to boost a child's self-esteem actually backfire?

Your job as a parent is not to create a happy child. If your child is temporarily unhappy, when she does choose to put a happy face back on, life will be better for all of you. After all, the long-term goal is to make her a responsible adult who doesn't think her happiness is the only thing that's important in life.

Many of us have unwittingly led our kids to think they're in the driver's seat of life, and that everyone else has to do their bidding—moms in particular. If you're a mom and you feel like a slave, exhausted by the end of the day, you especially need this participant's guide. You deserve more, and so do your kids.

If you want your child to emerge a healthy, contributing member of your family and society, *Have a New Kid by Friday Participant's Guide* will help you do just that—produce the kind of adult you'll be proud to call your son or daughter now and down the road. It'll ratchet down the stress level in your home and give you freedom you've never experienced before in your parenting.

Remember

- Your kids' game plan is to call the shots. But you don't have to let them.
- Nothing in life is a free ride. The sooner your kids learn that, the better.
- Your job as a parent isn't to create a happy child. It's to create a responsible adult.

My Game Plan for Today

1. Identify which child most needs to become a new kid by Friday. (Hint: When you think of this kid, your blood pressure skyrockets.)

2. Commit to the five-day Monday-to-Friday process.

Aha Moments

Prayer

- For my eyes to be open in a new way to my child's actions and my own.
- For stick-to-it willpower.
- For my friends in the group, who will share the same journey.

Monday

Where Did They All Come From?

Why do your kids do what they do—and continue to do it? Here's the secret you need to know.

The Kickoff

1. What is your number one challenge with your child right now?

2. How does your current response to that challenge impact your relationship with your child? What would you like your relationship to be like?

Watch

Watch "Monday—Where Did They All Come From?" on *Have a New Kid by Friday DVD*.

Discuss the DVD

1. If you have more than one child in your family, what are the things that they fight about most?

2. What are the specific techniques kids use to ramp up the battle between them?

3. How does learning that fighting is an act of cooperation (it takes two) change your perspective on how to respond to sibling rivalry? In what practical ways can you keep the ball of responsibility firmly in the squabbling children's court?

4. When do kids tend to have major meltdowns, like the four-year-old in the scene on the DVD who decided he wanted a treat?

5. When you identify a child's trigger point, how can you effectively throw him or her a curveball and provide a teachable moment?

6. Attention, power, and revenge are the three reasons a child will misbehave. Which one of these is best demonstrated by the four-year-old in the DVD? Why do you think that?

7. Why is it important for children to get attention—any kind of attention—whether positive or negative?

8. If you had to wake your child up and endure power struggles every morning, would you do what Dr. Leman suggested? Why or why not? What else would you try?

9. How can realizing that children are creatures of habit help you form game plans for success in changing their behavior?

Taking It Deeper

Why is it these days so many children diss their parents—and get away with it? And why are so many parents caught in the roles of threatening and cajoling and never getting anywhere?

It all comes down to who is really in charge of your family. Is it you or your child?

1. What is more important to you—to be your child's friend or to be their parent? Be honest. Explain.

2. Every child has a predictable strategy. In the daily game of trial and error, designed to get the best of you, he's motivated to win because then you'll do anything he says. That means if he tries something and it works, he'll try it again. But he'll ramp up the efforts a little. How have you seen this truth play out in your own home? Give an example of a recent real-life scene.

3. The esteemed psychiatrist Alfred Adler talked about the "purposive nature of the behavior." What proof do you see that when your child misbehaves, she's doing it to get your attention?

4. What are some ways to give your child attention for positive things he does?

5. Do you ever win in a power struggle with your child? Why or why not? Which of you has the most to lose? Explain.

6. What do the following Scriptures say about the roles that God gives to children? To parents?

> Children, obey your parents; this is the right thing to do because God has placed them in authority over you. Honor your father and mother. This is the first of God's Ten Commandments that ends with a promise. And this is the promise: that if you honor your father and mother, yours will be a long life, full of blessing. (Eph. 6:1–3 TLB)

Come, my children, listen to me;
    I will teach you the fear of the LORD. (Ps. 34:11)

7. Do you consider always telling a child what to do and making choices on her behalf disrespectful of her? Why or why not?

8. Why does asking questions sometimes backfire?

9. Go back to what you wrote or shared about your number one challenge with your child right now. How might you use the following principles to help with that situation?
   - Say it once.
   - Turn your back.
   - Walk away.

10. What proof do you see in your own children that they are creatures of habit? (For example, some night when you're tucking in one of your children, just leave out one part of the routine and watch your kid turn into Judge Judy: "Mommy, you forgot to rub my chin with my blankie. . . .") How might you use that truth of human nature in forming your game plan of having a new kid by Friday?

Parent, it's time for you to step up to the plate. Your child needs to know that you mean business—what you say is what you will do. You will not be dissed, and if you are, there will be consequences. Immediate consequences. And you will not be talked out of them.

Today's children need guidance. They need accountability. They need to be taught that there are consequences for their actions (or their inactions).

Remember

- Kids do what they do because they've gotten away with it.
- When you choose to do battle with your child, you'll never win.
- Say it once, turn your back, and walk away.

My Game Plan for Today

1. Observe what's going on in my house.

My notes:

2. Think about things that I want to change.

   My notes:

3. Decide to take the bull by the horns.

   My ideas:

4. Expect great things to happen.

   My dreams:

Aha Moments

Prayer

- For the courage to step up and be a parent, even when it's difficult.
- For the reminder not to follow my feelings (guilt, anger, etc.) but to choose my actions wisely.
- For my group members, as we uphold each other in accountability.

Tuesday

Disarming the Dude (or Dudette) with the 'Tude

Attitude, Behavior, and Character are the most important ABCs of all. You can teach them in a way your child will never forget.

The Kickoff

1. Which child do you butt heads with most in your family? Is that child the most like you or the least like you? Explain.

2. Which is more important to you: to say the right things or to do the right things? Or are they both important? Explain.

Watch

Watch "Tuesday—Disarming the Dude (or Dudette) with the 'Tude" on *Have a New Kid by Friday DVD*.

Discuss the DVD

1. Have you ever wondered whether all the things you do with and for your kids will make a difference? How does Dr. Leman's personal story encourage you to view current situations with your kids in a long-term perspective?

2. What are the top three concerns of parents? (Hint: Use the acronym ABC.)

3. Think back to the stories about the picky eater and the child potty training. How do we as parents sometimes up the ante on ourselves by catering too much to our kids?

4. What is "parental poker"? How might you play parental poker in a current situation with your kids?

5. Think about the story of the 11-month-old boy who liked to pull books off the bookshelf. How can you tell the difference between

disobedience and age-appropriate behavior? Between defiance and simply an accident?

6. Which of the three simple strategies for success do you most need to work on in order to have a new kid by Friday?
   • Let reality be the teacher.
   • Learn to respond rather than react.
   • B doesn't happen until A is completed.

   What steps might you take today in working on that strategy with your kids?

7. Think about the challenges you face with your kids. Which ones are mountains?

8. Which challenges are molehills—ones that won't matter in the long run?

9. How would you have responded if your teenage son came to the dinner table and announced he was getting an earring? How did Dr. Leman and his wife respond, and why? When should you let your kids dream, and when should you let reality do the talking?

10. Dr. Leman makes the statements, "Kids are always looking up. They're taking emotional notes, spiritual notes, on how we live our lives," and "With character, you are who you are. And don't think kids don't know the difference between who you say you are and who you really are." How do these statements provide perspective for the way you think about your kids and the way you'll respond to the curveballs they throw you?

Taking It Deeper

When it comes to disrespect, how do you know what's normal, what's "just a phase," and what's an attitude to be dealt with?

Almost 100 percent of the time parents *know the difference* between respect and getting dissed, but they choose to ignore it. Why would they do that? Because many parents today want to be their child's friend. But this never works in the long run.

Kids are kids. Just accept the fact that they'll say and do the dumbest, most embarrassing things you can imagine. As 1 Corinthians 13:11 says,

"When I was a child, I talked like a child, I thought like a child, I reasoned like a child. When I became a man, I put childish ways behind me." Every child will fail and make mistakes. But there's a big difference between being dumb and exhibiting disrespect.

1. Think back to the last time your child misbehaved (for some of you, that will be just minutes). Ask yourself, "What is the purposive nature of the behavior?" (In other words, why is your child doing what he does? What does he have to gain by such behavior?)

2. How did that behavior make you as a parent feel? (What you think about the situation and the emotions you generate have everything to do with the way you respond to the situation.)

3. As you look back on the situation, would you consider it a mountain (something that will matter in the long run) or a molehill (something that will take care of itself or is a small concern in the grand scheme of what you're trying to accomplish in your child's life)? Did your response match appropriately? If so, how? If not, why not?

4. How can asking yourself the three questions—"What is the purposive nature of the behavior?" "How does the behavior make me as a parent feel?" and "Is this situation a mountain or a molehill?"—put any of your child's behaviors (or misbehaviors) in perspective? And perhaps even change your feelings?

5. Attitude is the entrée into a child's head and heart. What your child thinks about herself—how she views herself and what happens to her—speaks loudly through her behavior. What does your child's behavior say about how she views herself right now?

6. What issues have led to the way your child feels about herself? How might you sensitively address them with her? Brainstorm here.

7. Kids catch attitude faster than anything. Take an honest look at your own attitude. Does it mirror your child's in any way? If so, how?

8. "Character is what really counts. It's who you are when no one is looking." Do you agree with this statement? Why or why not?

9. How can you encourage and reinforce good character traits in your kids in a natural, positive way? What hints does the following verse give? "Impress them on your children. Talk about them when you sit at home and when you walk along the road, when you lie down and when you get up" (Deut. 6:7).

10. Proverbs 22:6 says, "Train a child in the way he should go, and when he is old he will not turn from it." What wisdom and encouragement does this provide about the time you as mom or dad spend in the trenches with your kids every day?

Your attitude has everything to do with how you live your life. It has everything to do with how you behave. And it has everything to do with the character you develop. What kids see in you is what they will model in their own lives. As you work together on Attitude, Behavior, and Character, you can work toward a relationship that's mutually satisfying.

Remember

- The key to changing your child's attitude is to change your own.
- Learn to distinguish mountains from molehills.
- Character is not only everything, it's the only thing.

My Game Plan for Today

Answer the following questions:

1. If I'm being honest with myself, what are my attitudes toward my kids?

2. How does my behavior on a daily basis reveal those attitudes?

3. What changes do I need to make in my behavior toward my kids in order for them to want to change how they behave?

4. What kind of character do I want to be known for? How can I get there?

Aha Moments

Prayer

- For God to reveal any blinders I might be wearing concerning my attitudes and actions.
- For clarity of thought and humility to make changes.
- For each member of the group, as we work toward becoming people of godly character.

Wednesday

*Show Me a Mean Teacher,
and I'll Show You a Good One
(It's All in the Perspective)*

Who do you want your child to be 5, 10, 15, 20 years down the road? What kind of parent do you want to be? With determination and three simple strategies for success, you can get there.

The Kickoff

1. If you could choose only three qualities for your child to develop and carry throughout life, what would they be? Why?

2. What steps can you take now to encourage these qualities in your child?

Watch

Watch "Wednesday—Show Me a Mean Teacher, and I'll Show You a Good One" on *Have a New Kid by Friday DVD*.

Discuss the DVD

1. What is the "authoritarian" parenting style—the one most common for people to have experienced growing up? What is it really saying to kids?

2. How do authoritarian parents sometimes misuse parental and scriptural authority, including verses such as, "Children, obey your parents" (Col. 3:20)? What long-term effects does this have on children, reaching even into their adult lives?

3. What is the "permissive" parenting style? How does it treat children, and what are the results both now and far down the road?

4. What is the "authoritative" parenting style? What benefits does it provide for both parent and child?

5. What happens in the parent-child relationship when you hold your child responsible and accountable for his or her actions?

6. Do you agree with Josh McDowell's statement, "Rules without relationship lead to rebellion"? Why or why not?

7. Has establishing rules worked in your house? If so, how? If not, why not? Give an example of a recent situation.

8. Imagine that today you switch to an authoritative parenting style. What immediate changes would you see in the atmosphere of your home? In the tension level? In your relationship with your children?

Taking It Deeper

Have you ever heard someone say, "I never wanted to be like my parents. I hated the way they parented. But then I open my mouth and sound just like them. And I act like it too!" This just goes to show that what parents model sticks—and sticks well. That's because every child longs for parental approval and can't stand it when he or she doesn't get it.

1. What kind of parenting style did you grow up with?
   - Authoritarian: "It's my way—my way only—or the highway. I'm in charge here."
   - Permissive: "Oh, honey, anything you want to do is fine with me. I'm your doormat."
   - Authoritative: "As parent and child, we are both equal in God's eyes. But we play differing roles. I am responsible for your well-being until you become an adult."

   How did that parenting style influence your own parenting style today?

2. How did your experience with your parents in your growing-up years influence how you think about or approach God?

3. If you are an authoritarian parent, what steps can you take to balance your tendencies to:
   - make all decisions for your child?
   - use reward and punishment to control your child's behavior?
   - always have to be right?
   - see yourself as better than your child just because you're the adult?
   - run your home with an iron hand?

4. If you are a permissive parent, what steps can you take to balance your tendencies to:
   - become a slave to your child?
   - place a higher priority on your child than your spouse (if you're married)?
   - provide your child with the "Disneyland" experience, making things as easy as possible?
   - invite rebellion with inconsistent parenting?

5. First Corinthians 13:4–5, 7–8 provides this "bucket list" of what love looks like:

   > Love is patient, love is kind. It does not envy, it does not boast, it is not proud. It is not rude, it is not self-seeking, it is not easily angered, it keeps no record of wrongs. . . . It always protects, always trusts, always hopes, always perseveres. Love never fails.

   How does this list stack up to the authoritative parenting style?

6. In Ephesians 6:4, God gives fathers a special responsibility: "Do not exasperate your children." Why do you think that instruction is given to fathers in particular?

7. Why is connecting with your child's heart the most important thing you can do—both now and in the long run?

8. How might you slip your child a commercial today? Do some brainstorming.

9. Psalm 127:3 says, "Sons are a heritage from the LORD, children a reward from him." How might these words encourage you, even in the most difficult moments of parenting?

Life speeds by like sand drains through an hourglass. You can't afford not to take advantage of the time you have with your kids. If you want something, start with that end in mind, said Stephen Covey, the recently deceased bestselling author and business consultant. When you apply that principle to parenting, it means that if you want your child to be kind to others in the future, teach your child to be kind now. If you want your child to be a responsible adult, teach responsibility now. If you want your child to enjoy spending time with you, start now in setting aside unpressured time to spend together instead of getting caught up in the rat race of constant activity.

Sometimes your parenting job will be tedious and boring (like washing the same clothes over and over). Other times the pace will be breakneck, especially when your children are young, apt to get into danger, or involved in a lot of activities. Sometimes you'll be annoyed and angry. So will your kids.

But rest assured that what your children think about you in this moment isn't necessarily what they will think about you for life. If you are calm and consistent, and you always do what you say you're going to do, then you will earn their respect and trust.

Remember

- What your children think about you at any particular moment isn't necessarily what they will think about you for life.
- The kind of parent you are influences who your child is and what he or she does.
- Your child longs for a connection—a relationship—with you.

My Game Plan for Today

1. Identify my parenting style—authoritarian, permissive, or authoritative. How does that learned style influence how I communicate with my kids and how I respond to their behavior? (All of us, at one time or another, have said, "I'll never say that to my kids." Then not only do you say it, but you say it with the same tone and inflection that your mom or dad did.)

2. Evaluate how my children respond to my parenting style.

3. Jot down ideas to adapt my parenting style to be more balanced.

4. Brainstorm ways to emphasize relationship in our home.

Aha Moments

Prayer

- For myself, as I grapple with the kind of parent I am and work toward the kind of parent I want to be.
- For my child, that God will give me creative ideas to connect relationally with him or her.
- For all group members to develop a godly perspective and take the "long view" in their relationships.

Thursday

But What If I Damage Their Psyche?
(Uh . . . What's a Psyche?)

Kids need Acceptance, Belonging, and Competence—the pillars of self-esteem. But there's a big difference between praise and encouragement.

The Kickoff

1. What are your top three expectations for your child right now?

2. On a scale of 1 to 10, how important is it to you that your child "feels good" about himself or herself? Explain.

Watch

Watch "Thursday—But What If I Damage Their Psyche?" on *Have a New Kid by Friday DVD*.

Discuss the DVD

1. What are the three ABCs that every parent must master? Why are they so important?

2. Why are we so driven as a society to throw around labels, such as ACA, OCD, ADD, and ADHD? What do the labels accomplish?

3. How do you see the truths of birth order—that all your kids are different, and that when your firstborn turns right, your secondborn will turn left—played out in your own family?

4. What are the character traits you see in:
   - firstborns

   - secondborns

- babies of the family

5. Why do parents always call on firstborn children when they want to get a job done? How might this lead to many of them becoming leaders in life? How can you encourage the best in your firstborn?

6. Why do middle children often feel "lost in the middle"? How can you encourage the best in your middle child?

7. How can you encourage responsibility in your baby of the family?

8. Why is it important to expect the best of your children and to avoid comparing them to each other?

9. Why does treating every child equally sound so good, when in practice, it's the wrong thing to do?

10. Why is it so important that your child feels accepted and knows she belongs to your family, and that you view her as competent?

Taking It Deeper

If you go out of your way to clear life's roads for your child—to do things for him that he should be doing for himself—you might think you're helping him with his self-esteem. But what are you really doing? Sending a negative message: "I think you're so stupid that you can't do it yourself . . . so I'll do it for you."

And if you remind kids more than once, you're saying, "You're so dumb I don't think you're going to get it, so I'll say it again." Actually, saying it once consistently increases your chance that you'll be heard and your instructions followed.

Every child lives up to the expectation you have for him or her.

1. What things do you think are important to do for children? What things should they do for themselves? Where do you draw the line as a parent on what to do and what not to do?

2. How do you decide where to set the bar for your child? What does it have to do with where your parents set the bar for you?

3. Dr. Leman likes to say, "An unhappy child is a healthy child." Do you agree? Why or why not?

4. When are you motivated to change something in your life? How can you apply this insight to parenting your children?

5. What's the difference between feeling good and having self-worth?

6. How can you show your child unconditional acceptance yet also hold her accountable for her actions? Brainstorm some ideas based on a situation that's happening in your home right now.

7. What's the difference between praise and encouragement? How can you model encouragement in your own home? What might you say to your child today, for starters?

8. What do the following verses say about praise, encouragement, and reward?

> Give her the reward she has earned,
>   and let her works bring her praise at the city gate. (Prov. 31:31)

> I do not accept praise from men. (John 5:41)

> Therefore encourage one another and build each other up, just as in fact you are doing. (1 Thess. 5:11)

> Encourage your hearts and strengthen you in every good deed and word. (2 Thess. 2:17)

If you want to empower your children, accept and love them unconditionally and provide opportunities for responsibility.

Make your relationship a priority over activities that take you away from home. If there is no sense of belonging in your home, there will be no relationship, and your children will be drawn toward acceptance and belonging in a group outside your home.

Give your children responsibility and encourage their efforts so they feel proud of their accomplishments. Praise links a child's worth to what he or she does; encouragement emphasizes the act. When you say, "Good job," what does that child think? *Hey, I can do this. My mom and dad believe I can do it. They're thinking the best of me. So let's see what I can do.*

Parent, you matter much more in your child's world than you think!

Remember

- Expect the best, get the best.
- To empower your child, accept and love them unconditionally and provide opportunities for responsibility.
- Praise links a child's worth to what he or she does; encouragement emphasizes the act.

My Game Plan for Today

Brainstorm ways to:

1. Show my child unconditional Acceptance.

2. Emphasize Belonging in our family.

3. Spur my child on to Competence.

4. Encourage—rather than praise—my child.

Aha Moments

Prayer

- For myself, as I empower my children through the ABCs—the three pillars of self-esteem—in my home.
- For the nudge I need as a reminder to change my praise to encouragement when I open my mouth.
- For my colleagues, as we learn from each other's successes and failures how to be godly parents.

Friday

The Doc Is In . . . and It's You

Today is the day you pull your game plan together. Your mantra: "I can't wait for that kid to misbehave, because I'm ready!"

The Kickoff

1. As you launch your game plan for having a new kid by Friday, what is the one thing that will be most difficult for you to do—the thing you'll have to stick to your guns about? Why?

2. Knowing you're weak or tend to back down in that area, what can you do now to prepare?

Watch

Watch "Friday—The Doc Is In . . . and It's You" on *Have a New Kid by Friday DVD*.

Discuss the DVD

1. Why is it so important for you as a parent to believe in your kid—and in who he is and the person he is capable of becoming?

2. Why is a "sneak attack" better than explaining the game plan to your kids?

3. "Warnings are disrespectful acts." Do you agree with that statement? Why or why not?

4. Pick one situation that occurs frequently in your house (for example, your child not getting up when the alarm goes off or your child mouthing off to you). Answer the following three questions about that behavior.

   • What's the situation?

- If you were a shrink, how would you diagnose what's happening?

- What's the purposive nature of the behavior? In other words, what purpose does the behavior serve?

5. In the situations you know you'll face as you launch your plan, how can you let reality be the teacher? Be specific.

6. Do you tend to allow "slow leaks" to happen, or are you the type that forces a blowout? Explain.

7. What benefits are there to forcing a blowout?

8. Answer the following questions about the first situation you know you'll face.

- What would I normally do?

- What is the new, committed me going to do differently?

Taking It Deeper

I'll let you in on a secret. Sometimes you're too good a mother. You're too good a father. You do way too many things for your kids. On Friday, Fun Day, you need to level the playing ground, using the "B doesn't happen until A is completed" principle.

None of us are perfect. Your children need the three-pronged foundation of Acceptance, Belonging, and Competence in order to become healthy, functioning members of society. They also need the character building of truth-telling and encouragement, rather than the false and empty platform of praise. Most of all, they need consistency. They need a mom and/or a dad who will stand up and be a parent. Even if that means being Public Enemy Number One of your kids for a while.

1. Now that you know your particular parenting style, how can you approach the launching of your game plan as an authoritative parent?

2. Why is consistency your ace in the hole?

3. What do the following passages have to say about the process of teaching and training a child? About the benefits?

> Only be careful, and watch yourselves closely so that you do not forget the things your eyes have seen or let them slip from your heart as long as you live. Teach them to your children and to their children after them. (Deut. 4:9)

> So that you, your children and their children after them may fear the LORD your God as long as you live by keeping all his decrees and commands that I give you, and so that you may enjoy long life. (Deut. 6:2)

4. If your child is a powerful child, set in his patterns of behavior, what is he likely to do in response to your game plan? How can preparing for this solidify your resolve (and gain you a needed sense of humor?)

Getting Ready for Fun Day

Want a new kid by Friday?
Here's what it takes, in a Top 10 Countdown style.
(For a summary, see page 69.)

10. **Be 100 percent consistent in your behavior.**

    Think of it this way: you're trying to forge a new and different path in life. You're retraining your kid—and yourself—to behave differently. Your kid needs to know you mean business.

    Okay, I realize that none of us are going to be 100 percent consistent. The point is that you will pursue excellence (but not perfection) through being as consistent as humanly possible.

9. **Always follow through on what you say you will do.**

    No matter the circumstances, what you say is what you do. Never ever back down. Don't be a wuss. It won't gain either you or your child anything. In fact, it will put you in an adversarial position with your child, who will wonder, *Hey, when is she serious, and when isn't she?*

8. **Respond, don't react.**

    Use actions, not words. Flying loose with your words will only gain you trouble. So close your mouth, think, and respond to the situation rather than reacting to it.

7. **Count to 10 and ask yourself, "What would my old self do in this situation? What should the new me do?"**

    Let's say the siblings in your home have been going after each other for nine years. What do you usually say and do? What will the new you do differently?

6. **Never threaten your kids.**

    The problem with threats is that our children know we don't mean them, because we rarely follow through on them. Even more, our threats often don't make sense: "All right, no more candy for life!" "If you don't stop standing on that chair, you're going to break your neck!" Even the youngest child can figure out when there's no action or truth behind the threats.

5. Apologize quickly when you get angry.

As soon as you get angry, you'll be back at square one. I understand that there are triggers—things your kids do that make you angry. But you're the adult in the situation. You are the one who ultimately decides when you get angry. Don't let your children control your moods. An explosion of anger is like throwing up all over your child. The release in tension may feel good temporarily, but look what you've done to your child.

Okay, so you're human. If and when you get angry, apologize quickly. For example: "Honey, I'm sorry. I shouldn't have said that."

4. Don't give any warnings.

If you warn your child, you're saying, "You're so stupid, I have to tell you twice." Your goal is to get your children to listen once, hear what you have to say, and act on it.

3. Ask yourself, "Whose problem is this?"

Don't own what isn't yours, and don't force the ownership on a sibling either. You need to keep the tennis ball in your child's court. Don't take over what she should be doing herself.

2. Don't think the misbehavior will go away.

I've got news for you. Kids won't stop misbehaving on their own. They gain too much by it. You have to intercede and administer loving and consistent discipline. You as a parent are responsible for informed guidance. In other words, you can't let the prisoners run the asylum.

1. Keep a happy face on, even when you want to . . . do something else.

Let's face it. We all have our days. But remember that you're the adult here.

5. Do a little dreaming. As you forge a new and different path for your relationship with your child, what do you hope to accomplish?

If you stick with the *Have a New Kid by Friday* plan, you'll get there!

Having a new kid by Friday isn't rocket science. Any parent can do it. Your kids need you to step up to the plate so life in your home can be the way it should be—a place of love, respect, and accountability.

The key to any action plan is consistency and follow-through. So many parents I've talked to say they've tried everything—spanking, taking away allowances, withholding privileges, etc. They've read all the books and consulted a bunch of experts, and nothing works.

But what they've been trying to do is like a frog jumping from lily pad to lily pad and never landing on any particular one for long. Is it any wonder that both children and parents are exasperated? So much confusion is created by the parents continually "switching the plan" to try to find something that works better.

The Leman strategy is simple. Say it once. Turn your back. Walk away. Let reality be the teacher. Learn to respond rather than react. B doesn't happen until A is completed.

It'll win the game every time. Guaranteed.

Remember

- If your child is thrashing like a fish out of water, you'll know you're on the right track.
- Don't own problems that aren't yours.
- Always follow through on what you say you will do.

My Game Plan for Today

1. After reading "Have a New Kid by Friday Plan for Success" (Appendix 1, pp. 67–68), which sessions do I want to reread to make sure I've accomplished the goals listed for each one?

2. What mountains do I want to address?

3. How do I usually react to stressful situations with and demands from my kids? How will I respond now?

   - For example, a situation that happens over and over in our home is:

   - What I usually say:

   - How I'll respond now that I can think through the plan in advance:

4. Which of the 10 points in "Getting Ready for Fun Day" (pp. 60–61) pose the greatest challenge to me personally? Why?

5. Get ready, get set . . . go!

Aha Moments

Prayer

- For remaining calm and rational, not owning what isn't mine, and having a sense of humor.
- For the focus and ability to stick with the plan . . . no matter what is slung my way.
- For each member in the group, as we get ready mentally and emotionally for Fun Day.

Epilogue

It's Time to Launch

You're armed with the *Have a New Kid by Friday* strategies and ready to tackle those things about your child and your relationship that drive you crazy. You know why they do what they do, and that the volume and continuation of their war whoops have to do with you and the kind of parent you've been. And you're convinced more than ever that Attitude, Behavior, and Character are what really matter both now and in the long run.

For some of you, sparking that change using the *Have a New Kid by Friday* game plan may be fairly easy. Five days in the saddle and your children will be so bamboozled by the change in you that their mouths will be agape. *Why doesn't that work anymore?* they'll wonder. *It always used to get me what I want. . . .*

For others of you, *Have a New Kid by Friday* will set the stage for how your family will now be run, but your child may be more resistant, more set in his or her ways. The younger the child, the easier it is to mold that wet cement. Usually the older the child, the more difficult he or she is to shape, because some of the prints of Attitude, Behavior, and Character have already begun to harden.

Since you've begun this participant's guide, some of you may have already had some great successes. You've seen the tremendous power you can have as a parent in creating the kind of environment that encourages your child to reach his or her true potential.

Others of you have battled difficult situations with a child who was extremely rebellious and gave you all kinds of worries and sleepless nights. At last your child has turned the corner. Let me issue you a word of caution. Don't get smug or think you have all of life's answers in your back pocket. And especially don't get out your shovel and start being a bone digger. Leave the past buried in the past. Just be thankful that both you and your child have a new grasp on life.

You see, you're not perfect, and neither is your child. Sometimes your child will misbehave—and in colorful, exasperating, and embarrassing ways. Sometimes *you* will be the one who gives in when you know you shouldn't, or the one who reverts to the old parenting style you grew up with. None of us are perfect, but the old adage is right: sometimes love has to be tough. And sometimes you have to be the one to deliver that type of love. Don't be afraid to let your kids know that you are very unhappy about a certain behavior or situation. Kids really do want to please you. The cubs in your family den don't like it when Mama Bear or Papa Bear is upset. So if you show tough love, the payoff will happen right in front of your eyes. You'll be amazed!

Today is *your day*. FUN DAY. The reward for your work and determination. The day you get to sit back and watch the FUN! The look of absolute confusion on your child's face when you launch your action plan will be priceless.

Your mantra should be, "I can't wait for that kid to misbehave, because I'm ready."

You too can experience what thousands of families already have: a complete revolution in their relationships and family life.

And with it comes a promise: "Oh, that their hearts would be inclined to fear me and keep all my commands always, so that it might go well with them and their children forever!" (Deut. 5:29).

Appendix 1

Have a New Kid by Friday
Plan for Success

Introduction

Identify what you'd like to change, and commit to this five-day plan.

Monday

In order for your child to know you mean business (and to keep you calm and rational):

- Say it once.
- Turn your back.
- Walk away.

Tuesday

It's all about the ABCs:

- Attitude
- Behavior
- Character

You understand where your child's attitudes came from, and you've done a check in the mirror for your own attitude. You understand why it's important to be aware of the purposive nature of your child's behavior. You're determined to hold firm in directing your child's character.

You also have the three simple strategies for success firmly in your mind:

- Let reality be the teacher.
- Learn to respond rather than react.
- B doesn't happen until A is completed.

Wednesday

You're taking the long view in this journey of parenting. You've evaluated the kind of parent you are:

- Authoritarian
- Permissive
- Authoritative or responsible

You've evaluated how your parenting style influences the way your children respond to you. You are actively thinking of ways your Attitude, Behavior, and Character can be better balanced in regard to your children.

You've decided to focus first on your relationship with your child, realizing that without relationship, any rules will not be effective.

You've also decided not to make mountains out of molehills, and you're strategizing which areas really are important ones to address.

Thursday

You understand the difference between self-esteem ("feeling good" about yourself) and true self-worth. You're evaluating how you can help your child develop the three pillars of self-worth:

- Acceptance
- Belonging
- Competence

You're determined to move from praise (focusing on how "good" a person is) to encouragement (focusing on an action).

Friday

This is the day you go for it—you launch your game plan. Remember, there are no warnings, no threats, no explanations—only action and follow-through. Above all, there's no backing down, no caving in. Your child needs to know you mean business, or you won't accomplish anything.

Appendix 2

The Top 10 Countdown
to Having a New Kid by Friday

10. Be 100 percent consistent in your behavior.

9. Always follow through on what you say you will do.

8. Respond, don't react.

7. Count to 10 and ask yourself, "What would my old self do in this situation? What should the new me do?"

6. Never threaten your kids.

5. Apologize quickly when you get angry.

4. Don't give any warnings. (If you warn your child, you're saying, "You're so stupid, I have to tell you twice.")

3. Ask yourself, "Whose problem is this?" (Don't own what isn't yours.)

2. Don't think the misbehavior will go away.

1. Keep a happy face on, even when you want to . . . do something else.

About Dr. Kevin Leman

An internationally known psychologist, radio and television personality, and speaker, **Dr. Kevin Leman** has taught and entertained audiences worldwide with his wit and commonsense psychology.

The *New York Times* bestselling and award-winning author of *Have a New Kid by Friday*, *Have a New Husband by Friday*, *Have a New You by Friday*, *Sheet Music*, and *The Birth Order Book* has made thousands of house calls through radio and television programs, including *Fox & Friends*, *The View*, Dr. Bill Bennett's *Morning in America*, Fox's *The Morning Show*, *Today*, *The 700 Club*, *Oprah*, CBS's *The Early Show*, *In the Market with Janet Parshall*, *Live with Regis Philbin*, CNN's *American Morning*, *Life Today* with James Robison, and *Focus on the Family*. Dr. Leman has also served as a contributing family psychologist to *Good Morning America*.

Dr. Leman is the founder and president of Couples of Promise, an organization designed and committed to help couples remain happily married. His professional affiliations include the American Psychological Association, the American Federation of Television and Radio Artists, and the North American Society of Adlerian Psychology.

In 2003, the University of Arizona awarded Dr. Leman the highest award they can give to one of their own: the Distinguished Alumnus Award. In 2010, North Park University awarded him an honorary Doctor of Humane Letters degree.

Dr. Leman received his bachelor's degree in psychology from the University of Arizona, where he later earned his master's and doctorate degrees. Originally from Williamsville, New York, he and his wife, Sande, live in Tucson, Arizona. They have five children and two grandchildren.

For information regarding speaking availability, business consultations, seminars, or the annual Couples of Promise cruise, please contact:

Dr. Kevin Leman
P.O. Box 35370
Tucson, Arizona 85740

Phone: (520) 797-3830
Fax: (520) 797-3809
www.birthorderguy.com
www.drleman.com

Resources by
Dr. Kevin Leman

Books for Adults

Have a New Kid by Friday
Have a New Husband by Friday
Have a New Teenager by Friday
Have a New You by Friday
The Birth Order Book
The Way of the Wise
What a Difference a Mom Makes
What a Difference a Daddy Makes
Under the Sheets
Sheet Music
Making Children Mind without Losing Yours
It's a Kid, Not a Gerbil!
Born to Win
Sex Begins in the Kitchen
7 Things He'll Never Tell You . . . But You Need to Know
What Your Childhood Memories Say about You
Running the Rapids
The Way of the Shepherd (written with William Pentak)
Becoming the Parent God Wants You to Be
Becoming a Couple of Promise
A Chicken's Guide to Talking Turkey with Your Kids about Sex
    (written with Kathy Flores Bell)
First-Time Mom
Step-parenting 101
Living in a Stepfamily without Getting Stepped On
The Perfect Match
Be Your Own Shrink
Stopping Stress before It Stops You
Single Parenting That Works
Why Your Best Is Good Enough
Smart Women Know When to Say No

Books for Children, with Kevin Leman II

My Firstborn, There's No One Like You
My Middle Child, There's No One Like You
My Youngest, There's No One Like You
My Only Child, There's No One Like You
My Adopted Child, There's No One Like You
My Grandchild, There's No One Like You

DVD/Video Series for Group Use

Have a New Kid by Friday
Making Children Mind without Losing Yours
    (Christian—parenting edition)
Making Children Mind without Losing Yours
    (Mainstream—public school teacher edition)
Value-Packed Parenting
Making the Most of Marriage
Running the Rapids
Single Parenting That Works
Bringing Peace and Harmony to the Blended Family

DVDs for Home Use

Straight Talk on Parenting
Why You Are the Way You Are
Have a New Husband by Friday
Have a New You by Friday

Available at
1-800-770-3830
or
www.drleman.com
or
www.birthorderguy.com

Visit DrLeman.com
for more information, resources, and videos from his popular books.

Follow Dr. Kevin Leman on

 Dr Kevin Leman

 drleman

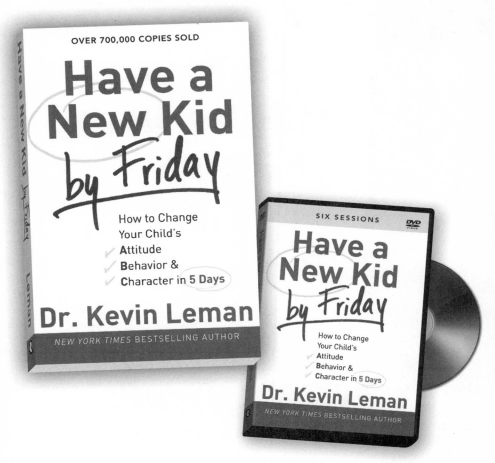

New York Times Bestselling Author
Dr. Kevin Leman
Will Help You with Real Change

Use these easy action plans to improve your family, communication, and life in five days!

Powerful kids
don't just happen.

They're created, and their power comes in different packages.
Whether loud and temperamental, quiet and sensitive, or stubborn
and manipulative, powerful children can make living with them a
challenge. But it doesn't have to be that way.

Kid-tested,
parent-approved

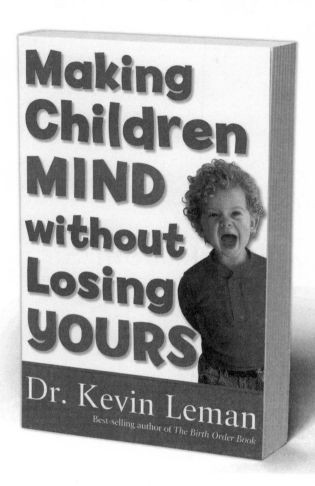

If anyone understands why children behave the way they do, it's Dr. Kevin Leman. In this bestseller he equips parents with seven principles of reality discipline—a loving, no-nonsense parenting approach that really works.

Be the First to Hear about Other New Books from REVELL!

Sign up for announcements about new and upcoming titles at

RevellBooks.com/SignUp

Don't miss out on our great reads!

Revell

a division of Baker Publishing Group
www.RevellBooks.com